What Lives Under the Carpet?

John Woodward

ReD KiTE

First published in the UK in 2000 by Red Kite,
an imprint of Haldane Mason Ltd
59 Chepstow Road
London W2 5BP

Reprinted 2002

ISBN 1-902463-23-4

A HALDANE MASON BOOK

Editors: Beck Ward and Ben Keith
Designer: Phil Ford
Picture Research: Ben Keith

Colour reproduction by CK Litho Ltd, UK

Printed in China

Picture Acknowledgements
Ardea London Ltd: /John Mason 19; **Bruce Coleman Collection:** /Kim Taylor 13, 23b, /Gerald S. Cubitt 36;
Natural History Museum: 25, 26; **NHPA:** /G.J. Cambridge 18; /Daniel Heuclin 32; /Stephen Dalton 38t, 39;
/Ron Fotheringham 40; /Anthony Bannister 41; **Oxford Scientific Films:** /London Scientific Films 8; 9; /G.I.
Bernard 11, 15l, 20; /Barrie E. Watts 12l, 12r; /J.A.L. Cooke 21; /Alastair Shay 27t; /David G. Fox 27b; /Scott
Camazine 29, 42; /Peter Clarke, Survival Anglia 34; /Harold Taylor 37b; Frithjof Skibbe 38b; /David Shale 43b;
Planet Earth Pictures: /André Bartschl 33; **Science Photo Library:** /Andrew Syred 4, 10, 22, 43t; /Eye of
Science 5, 17, 24t, 24b, 30, 31b, 37t; /Dr Tony Brain 6, 35; /Biophoto Associates 7; /Cath Wadford 14; /Martin
Dohrn 15r; /Dr Morley Read 16; /Jane Shemilt, Cosine Graphics 23t; /David Scharf 28l; 28r; /K.H. Kjeldsen 31t.

Contents

Introduction

A few thousand years ago, humans were just part of the wildlife. We lived out in the open, hunting and gathering foods such as berries and nuts. Then, some bright spark invented farming and we stopped roaming around the landscape and started living in houses.

The earliest houses were just shacks, but gradually we learned how to make them water-proof, wind-proof, cold-proof, everything-proof. There may be freezing rain outdoors, but the climate inside a centrally-heated house is like a warm desert. We can create our own little world, which seems to have nothing to do with the real world outside. Wildlife is just something you watch on TV.

Or is it? The snug houses we live in can make comfortable homes for other animals too. They sneak in when we're not looking and some of them never leave. If they're big enough we might notice them and chase them out, but smaller creatures like insects and spiders can hide in dark corners and crevices. They are doing so right now, as you read this.

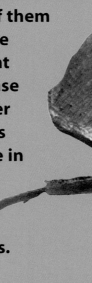

Bloodthirsty critter! Bedbugs live on a diet of human blood.

BUG ALERT!

Stowaways

Some of the animals that live in our houses can barely survive outdoors. They were once accidentally imported from warmer parts of the world and they now live in our centrally-heated cities. They also live in ships, trains and aircraft, and legend has it one cockroach even stowed away aboard the Apollo XII spacecraft that went to the moon! So they are still being carried around the globe, and many of the creatures you'll meet in this book are now found all over the world.

Your personal zoo

How many creatures share your house? It depends on what sort of house it is, where it is, and how you live. An old, damp house in the woods usually has more kinds of creature than a centrally-heated high-rise apartment in the city. On the other hand, city apartments may get invaded by huge numbers of one particular type of insect – the cockroach.

Many animals are just looking for warmth and shelter, and are no trouble at all. Most of the real pests are attracted by food left lying around, so clean, tidy habits can help keep them out. The vacuum cleaner is a real help here, clearing up crumbs of food as well as smaller pests like fleas and dust mites. But however hard you try, you'll never get rid of them all.

Don't panic!

As you read this book, you may get the idea that your house is overrun with wildlife – most of it dangerous, disgusting or both. Don't panic! Most houses have only a few of these creatures living in them, and usually they are fairly harmless. You'll probably never see any of the venomous ones, but they're worth knowing about, just in case . . .

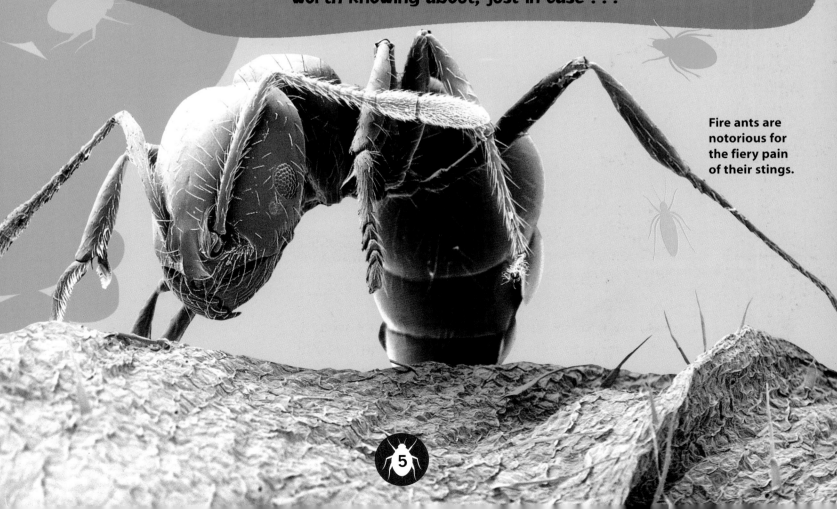

Fire ants are notorious for the fiery pain of their stings.

What Lives Under the Carpet?

Back in the bad old days of the Middle Ages, floors were often strewn with rushes to soak up mud, spilled food and worse. All kinds of creatures lived down there, feasting on food remains and on each other. It could get quite disgusting, but now and again the rushes and their resident animals were thrown on the dump and replaced. It was like a disposable carpet.

Today, our carpets are permanent. They stretch from wall to wall and are nailed down so you can't even pick them up and shake them. You can attack them with a vacuum cleaner, but a lot of the dirt stays. Small animals nestling between the fibres may stay put too, clinging on tight as the vacuum cleaner tornado passes. Some eat debris, while others feed on the carpet itself. More worryingly, some might like to feed on you!

Warm as toast

A carpet can get really warm, especially near a fireplace. This may not suit most animals, but it's perfect for an odd little creature called the firebrat. It's a very simple insect with a long, flexible body and no wings. It is able to eat almost anything and it loves to be hot, sneaking out of its refuge in the carpet to bask in the heat of the fire – just like a tiny cat.

Carpet beetles never have a bad hair day – they just eat it!

Woolly bears

Some modern carpets are made from artificial plastic fibre but other carpets are knotted from tough wool. This makes a tasty meal for some amazing insects that can actually eat it. These carpet beetle grubs are known as woolly bears because of their fur coats. They have special chemicals in their stomachs that convert wool into sugar, so if you give them the chance they'll munch through your wool carpet as if it were cotton candy.

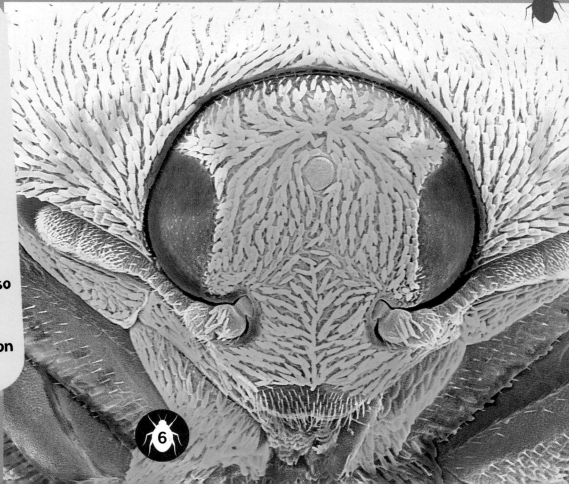

Cat cargo

If you have a cat, then it probably picks up fleas. When the cat comes into the house, fleas often jump off and burrow into the carpet. If they find a snug corner, out of reach of the vacuum cleaner, they breed. Their maggot-like young feed on debris in the carpet, until they turn into bloodsucking adults.

There are all sorts of fleas. They include hedgehog fleas, dog fleas, penguin fleas and even a Tasmanian devil flea! Each likes to suck the blood of its own special animal, but if it's really hungry it will try almost anything. For a cat flea, the next best thing to a cat is its owner, and that means you.

Your blood could make a savoury snack for a hungry cat flea.

Rocket flea

Jumping is very important to a flea. It has spring-loaded back legs that can be cocked like a gun, so when the flea flicks the trigger they catapult it into the air at about 20 times the speed of a guided missile. A tiny cat flea can jump over 34 cm (11 in) – about 250 times its own length. That's like a human jumping over a skyscraper!

Fleabytes

- The bubonic plague that killed millions of people was caused by a microbe carried in the blood of rats. The microbe was picked up by rat fleas, who passed it on to people.
- There is a flea that feeds mainly on humans rather than animals. Luckily, it needs damp, dirty conditions to survive, and hates central heating.

Itch, scratch

Fleas have sharp mouthparts that punch into your skin like a tiny drill. After a while, their bites begin to itch and you'll start to scratch. The flea has tough armour, though, that makes it difficult to kill. But since it would rather live on your cat, it usually jumps back into the carpet after it has had its meal.

BUG ALERT!

TV roach

While you are sitting comfortably watching TV, something else might be watching you. Brown-banded cockroaches came over to America from Africa in the kit of returning soldiers. Since they were used to a tropical climate, they moved into houses to keep warm.

This bug has a talent for getting into televisions and other heat-producing electrical devices. Sometimes this 'TV roach' dies inside the set, and liquid leaks from its body, short-circuits the TV and destroys it.

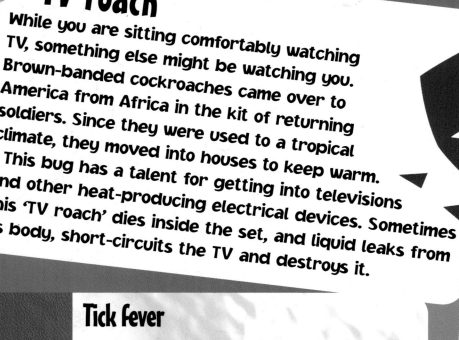

Tick fever

The problem with ticks is not the blood they take, but the diseases they can give you. Ticks carry more nasty microbes in their saliva than most other bloodsucking bugs put together, and some of them are lethal.

The Rocky Mountain wood tick, for example, may carry Colorado tick fever. If it's not treated in time, this disease kills eight out of every ten people who catch it, making it one of the most deadly on the planet.

BUG ALERT!

A tick's bite can be deadly, but only if it is carrying something nasty.

Assorted bloodsuckers

Fleas are not the only bloodsuckers that live on cats and dogs: there can be lice and ticks, too. Lice are tiny, flattened insects with strong claws that cling tightly to the hair of animals. They can't jump like fleas, so they are less likely to end up hiding in the carpet. But you never know!

Ticks are much more worrying. They are the tiny, bloodsucking relatives of spiders. A tick may stab your dog's skin with its barbed jaws, glue itself in place and feed for several days. When it is swollen with blood the tick drops off and may push its way down into the carpet. Perhaps its next meal will be human blood!

Walking nightmare

In Sydney, Australia, just visiting the fridge for a drink in the middle of the night can be a fatal mistake. As you pad across the living room carpet in bare feet, you risk a nightmare encounter with one of the deadliest animals on Earth: the Sydney funnelweb spider.

Funnelwebs are big, black, mean-looking spiders with huge fangs. Like most spiders, they kill their insect prey with venom, but for some reason the venom of the males contains a nerve poison that can kill people too.

They normally live in silk-lined burrows among rocks and soil, but on summer nights the males leave their burrows and set off in search of females. Since they often live near houses, the wandering males can sometimes get inside. And if they run into trouble as they cross the floor, they bite.

This funnelweb is about to pounce, so stay back!

Horror bite

When a funnelweb spider bites, it doesn't just give a nip and run away. It punches its fangs deep into its victim's flesh, biting again and again to inject as much venom as possible. Being bitten by a female is bad enough, but if the spider is a male its nerve poison soon gets to work, causing muscle spasms, sweating and sickness. Eventually you fall unconscious, and if you don't get to hospital quickly, you're dead.

Funnelweb facts

- Amazingly, a lot of animals are almost unaffected by a funnelweb spider's bite. For cats, rats and rabbits, the bite is no worse than a bee sting.
- Roaming funnelwebs often fall into swimming pools, but they can float around for hours and still bite.
- The spider's fangs are strong enough to punch right through your fingernail.

What Lives Under the Sink?

Most modern houses are bright, warm and dry, but there may be a few damp and dismal patches under the sink or behind the washing machine. These cool, clammy corners are just perfect for a bunch of equally cool, clammy customers who can't cope with the desert climate created by central heating.

Despite their name, earwigs have never lived in people's ears.

   They include creatures like the woodlouse (which we will meet later in the cellar), the pillbug and the fierce, leggy centipede. These animals are not insects, and they are not so well waterproofed. If they venture too far from their corners they start drying out, but they can usually manage to get far enough to find a meal. If the house is cold and damp they can travel much further, and, in the days before central heating, they lived all over the house.

BUG ALERT!

Expensive tastes

A damp kitchen corner is luxury accommodation for the slippery, glinting silverfish. This odd little insect has an amazing ability to digest the tough plant fibre known as cellulose: the stuff we use to make paper and cardboard. So as well as eating the food in the kitchen cupboard, the silverfish is often able to eat the packet too. It doesn't stop there. If conditions suit them, silverfish can spread right through the house, feeding on unlikely things like wallpaper, books and pictures. To a silverfish a library is a restaurant, and a priceless work of art is just lunch.

Tight squeeze

Although it's mainly a garden animal, the pincer-tailed earwig often finds its way into the house. It hates light, so it crawls into the darkest, tightest corner it can find. When it can feel both its back and belly pressed against something, it feels safe and stops moving.

Earwiggery

- You can tell the sex of an earwig from its pincers. If they're curved like two halves of a circle, it's a male. If they're almost straight, it's a female.
- An earwig can fly, using wings that it keeps beneath tiny protective covers on its back. They have to be folded into about 40 layers to fit, and all that folding takes so long that the earwig usually prefers to walk.

Fast and Furious

Little animals like the silverfish might feel safe in their dark, damp corners, but they are wrong. Their musty lairs also attract a creature that is as deadly to small insects as any spider: the multi-legged, poison-fanged centipede.

The centipede is a fast-moving killer that eats insects, spiders, woodlice, worms and even other centipedes. It chases after its prey with furious energy – pouncing and biting with a set of curved, hollow fangs that inject a paralysing venom. The poison works almost instantly, stunning the poor animal so it is helpless to stop the hungry centipede from eating it alive.

The centipede has an instinct for creeping into tight, dark crevices during the day, just like the earwig. Sometimes it finds an earwig already installed, but that's too bad for the earwig.

Legarhythmics

Some centipedes really do have more than 100 legs, but the common centipede has only 30. Even so, that's a lot of legs! You might think it would keep tripping over itself, but the centipede avoids this by moving its legs in strict sequence, one after the other. As the legs bunch together and then spread apart again, waves of movement ripple down each side of its body. It certainly works – just try catching one!

With all those legs, of course centipedes can run fast!

Little armadillos

One of the more entertaining animals that lives in damp places is the little pillbug. Scientists know it as *Armadillidium*, and if you upset it, you'll see why. It rolls itself up in an armoured ball like a tiny armadillo, with its legs and feelers packed inside. The tough shell protects it against most of its enemies, including the centipede, and you can roll it about like a pill without doing it any harm.

Expendable legs

One of the leggier house visitors is a relative of the spiders called the harvestman. There are many different types, but they all have stumpy one-piece bodies, two eyes and eight outrageously long legs. If it runs into trouble, though, a harvestman can lose two, three or even four legs by deliberately snapping them off. It leaves its enemy clutching a leg or two while it makes a getaway.

Like centipedes, the harvestman is not very waterproof, so it dries out easily. It usually gets in the house by mistake, and if it can't get out again it must find a damp corner to survive. It feeds mainly on other animals, dead or alive, which it finds using smell sensors on its second pair of legs. If it loses both of these in an accident, it cannot find prey, and eventually starves.

Pillbugs: hard on the outside, soft in the middle.

Slugs 'n' snails

Most of the animals that lurk in clammy corners of the house disappear during the day, leaving no trace. Some are not so good at covering their tracks, though. You can sometimes see them glinting in the morning sun: silvery, slimy snail trails.

You might think the house has to be dripping wet to attract slugs and snails, but they can be surprisingly adventurous. Their trails often lead under the door, across the kitchen and into damp corners behind sinks and washing machines. Slugs rely on finding somewhere damp or they dry out and die, but a snail can shut itself in its shell. Small snails sometimes get stranded half-way up walls, imprisoned in their shells by the dry air all around them.

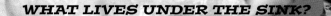

It might be far from home, but the oriental cockroach knows its way around our kitchens.

Oriental invader

Of all the creatures that live in dark kitchen corners, the ones we hate most are cockroaches. These beetle-like insects eat almost anything, including stored food that we might be meaning to eat ourselves. Not content with that, they spread oily fluids, tainting anything they don't actually eat with a foul smell.

There are several different types of cockroach. Some prefer damp places, including the oriental cockroach. This probably came from southern Asia or Africa back in the 16th century, but it has been carried all over the world by man. It lurks in basements, under sinks and behind cupboards, emerging at night to feed. It never flies – the female doesn't even have wings – but it can run very fast on its long, spiny legs.

Born survivors

Cockroaches have been part of the wildlife for over 300 million years and in all that time they have hardly changed at all. They are incredibly tough, able to survive weeks without water, all kinds of poisonous chemicals and even the explosion of a modest nuclear bomb. A headless cockroach was once seen to get up and start searching for a place to lay its eggs. Now that's survival!

BUG ALERT!

What Lives in the Larder?

The main reason why many small animals come and live in our houses is the food – our food. We spill it all over the place, and we keep great stocks of it in our fridges and store cupboards. A chilly, well-sealed fridge is difficult for animals to get into – which is one reason why we have fridges. A food store or larder, however, is easy.

If you open the larder door you can see the attraction. There's flour, rice and sugar; muesli, cereals and beans; raisins, currants, apricots and nuts – not to mention half-eaten loaves of bread, bags of crisps, cakes, pies and biscuits. Some of this stuff is tightly sealed in cans and packages, but some of it is just roughly wrapped. It's a feast, and a crowd of very small animals are probably enjoying it right now.

Biscuit beetles

During the late 18th century, the British sailors of Nelson's navy survived on a diet of cheese, salted meat and a bread substitute called ship's biscuit. On long voyages, these foods became infested with insects. The biscuit, in particular, was often crawling with tiny beetles related to the woodworm. The sailors had nothing else to eat, though, so they usually ate their biscuit ration in the dark, when they couldn't see the beetles.

If you leave biscuits, bread or flour lying around in your larder, you too could attract biscuit beetles. If you find them in your biscuit just as you're about to take a bite, you'll have some idea how it felt to be a sailor 200 years ago. They call it living history!

The tiny biscuit beetle added vitamins and protein to the diet of 18th-century sailors.

Roach record

In 1994–5, an American pest control company sponsored a competition for the six most cockroach-infested houses in the USA. One of the 'winners' was over-run by between 60,000 and 100,000 cockroaches and, not surprisingly, the family who lived there always slept with the lights on. The prize, by the way, was a free treatment with insecticide – a lot of insecticide!

High-rise roach

A kitchen cupboard full of food attracts hungry insects like a magnet, and few come hungrier than the German cockroach. If this smelly relative of the house cricket gets into the larder, it eats its way through as much food as possible and fouls the rest with its vile scent, just like any other cockroach.

It is much more adventurous than most, though, and it can take over entire houses, apartment blocks and even skyscrapers. In some high-rise buildings, German cockroaches have invaded the gaps between the girders and concrete, so the only way of getting rid of them is to call in the demolition squad.

The German cockroach likes midnight feasts.

Dedicated thief

One little beast has become so dedicated to stealing food from the larder that it is actually called the larder beetle. It's a variation of the carpet beetle, with furry young that can eat almost anything that was once alive. It has a close relative called the bacon beetle, and both lay their eggs on any stored meat they can find. When the eggs hatch, the beetle grubs eat voraciously until they turn into mature beetles, then fly away and lay eggs of their own.

Larder beetles eat anything from bacon to wool.

BUG ALERT!

Skipping lunch

Cheese is odd stuff. Basically, it's made from rotten milk, and some of the most expensive cheeses are mouldy!

Cheese has always been popular in Europe, though. In the past, one of the greatest treats for a connoisseur was a cheese that was literally alive with fly maggots. These were the young of the cheese skipper, a little black fly that laid its eggs on ham, bacon and cheese. The eggs hatch into small maggots that burrow through the cheese, eating as they go. They were supposed to improve the flavour of the cheese, so the more maggoty, the better. Mmmmm. . . .

But why are they called skippers? If they feel threatened, the maggots try to escape by bending their legless bodies like springs and leaping into the air. They can jump up to 15 cm (6 in) like this. Imagine them doing it as the cheese was about to be eaten – it makes the average cheese sandwich seem quite dull!

House crickets love to make music.

Musical pest

When most kitchens had big, iron, coal-fired stoves, there was always a warm corner for the house cricket. This chirpy character probably came from North Africa and the Middle East, and spread to cooler countries where it likes to find a warm spot indoors.

In the past, its favourite place was near a hot stove, and because of its musical song people sometimes treated it as a sort of pet. With central heating it has become more common, and more likely to turn up in the larder. Since it eats any stored food, it no longer seems so cute, and the pet has become a pest.

BUG ALERT!

Bookworm

One pest that seems to get everywhere is the little booklouse: a pale, soft-bodied insect that looks like a tiny breadcrumb on legs. It eats stored foods like flour and biscuits, as well as the glue used in old book covers. It's the original bookworm, and it can be quite a problem in libraries stuffed with ancient, rare books.

Most people come across it in the larder or kitchen when they disturb bags of flour or other foods, forcing it to run for cover. It hurtles along at a terrific rate, so while it may be a bookworm it's no couch potato.

Sweet discovery

If you leave anything sweet in the larder, such as a bowl of sugar or a sticky cake, it could easily attract the interest of an ant or two. Or four, eight, sixteen, thirty-two, sixty-four. . . . The fact is, there's no such thing as an ant or two. They live in colonies like bees, with thousands of worker ants looking after a single queen and her young. Any ant that discovers something delicious, like a sticky cake, goes back to the nest to tell the others, leaving a scent trail to show them the way. Before long, there may be a whole column of ants marching along the trail, eating their fill of cake and marching back again. The ants on their way back rub feelers with the new arrivals, maybe telling them that there's plenty of food left. When it's all gone, they tell them that, too, and they all turn around and go home – you hope!

Garbage disposal

When an animal dies out in the woods, its remains are soon disposed of by a host of flies and other insects. They lay their eggs on the carcass, and when the grubs hatch, they eat away the flesh until nothing is left but a few bones. It's a vital service because without them, the world would be knee-deep in dead bodies.

As far as flies are concerned, there's not much difference between a dead rabbit in the woods and a cooked chicken in the larder, so if they can, they'll buzz into the kitchen and dispose of that too. The main culprits are the metallic blue blow flies known as bluebottles, but you might get the odd greenbottle or grey flesh fly, too. Their white, carrot-shaped maggots burrow into the meat and liquefy it with their digestive juices. Within a few days, they are ready to crawl away and turn into adult flies themselves.

Flies are attracted to anything that smells bad.

What Lives in the Closet?

When did you last tidy your room? Just look at the state of the floor! What are you going to do about it? Exactly – pick it all up and sling it all into the closet! Be careful, though. There may be a few creatures in there that you don't want to disturb. Some are quite harmless, like sleeping butterflies and ladybirds in winter. They creep into the closet because it's dry and warm, and it seems like a good place to hide from the winter frost. Others can be more of a problem, because they actually eat the things you keep in there.

Most discouraging of all, though, are the creatures that take a bite out of you: the bloodsucking bugs and venomous spiders. A couple of these can really wreck your life, so you need to know about them. In the meantime, leave the closet door shut!

The house moth caterpillar has expensive tastes in clothing – your clothing!

Expensive tastes

The munching moth caterpillars in your closet often have to share their food with greedy beetle grubs: 'woolly bears' related to the ones that live in the carpet. They are known as wardrobe beetles and fur beetles. Like the moth caterpillars, they can digest wool, hair and dried skin, and they don't care whether it's part of a dead mouse, an old sock or a fur coat.

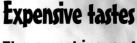

BUG ALERT!

Edible clothing

The most notorious closet creatures must be clothes moths. The moths themselves are no trouble; like many winged insects, they hardly eat at all. The real damage is caused by their caterpillars.

Out in the wild, these insects eat the dry skin and hair of dead animals after fly maggots have devoured all the flesh, making them useful waste disposal workers. Unfortunately, they can't tell the difference between a dead sheep and a lamb's-wool jumper, and why should they? It's all food, and if you leave anything woollen undisturbed in the closet for long enough, they'll eat it into holes. That goes for knitted pullovers, silk scarves and even fur coats.

Given the chance, the caterpillars will keep eating for about six weeks. Eventually, they turn into drab little moths, but by then the damage is done.

The ladybirds' bright colours warn enemies that they don't taste very nice.

Winter visitors

In countries with cold winters, many insects survive by finding dry, sheltered places where they can hide from the worst of the frost. They stop feeding, switch off and spend the winter months in a deep, deep sleep called hibernation. In spring they wake up, refuel and get on with their lives.

Some of these winter refugees come into the house, and may find their way into the bedroom or closet. Ladybirds often tuck themselves into crevices or the tight folds of curtains, and butterflies perch in corners where they hope not to be disturbed. Another common winter visitor is the green lacewing, a fragile-looking creature that is actually a fierce hunter of greenfly and other pests. They're no trouble, so leave them be!

Big mistake

To an insect, spending the winter in your house might seem like a good idea. After all, it's warm and dry, and many insects make a good living eating the food we leave lying around.

In fact, hibernating indoors can be a big mistake. It worked well enough when houses had plenty of dark, cold, undisturbed corners, but such places are scarce in these days of electric lights and central heating. If it is roused by warmth and light, a butterfly wastes precious energy flying around. It can look for food to replace the energy, but since it feeds from flowers, it is wasting its time indoors. If the butterfly finds another dark corner it may fall asleep again, but its fuel supplies may have drained so low that it never wakes up.

Plague bug

Most insects are no real trouble. They might sting you, ruin your food or eat holes in your clothes, but you can live with that. The insects you really have to worry about are the ones that can kill you.

Every year, half a million people in Latin America catch an infection called chagas disease. About 45,000 of these – mostly children – die within a few weeks. The rest suffer years of illness and then most die of heart failure. It's a plague, and like the great plagues of history, it's carried by an insect: the bloodsucking chagas bug.

Chagas bugs live all over tropical America – many houses in country areas are infested with them. During the day they hide in dark crevices and corners, but at night they emerge to look for food: blood. They attack while you sleep, then creep away. You wake up with an itchy bite, and maybe that's all. If you're unlucky, though, the bug may be one of the infected ones, and then you're in deep trouble.

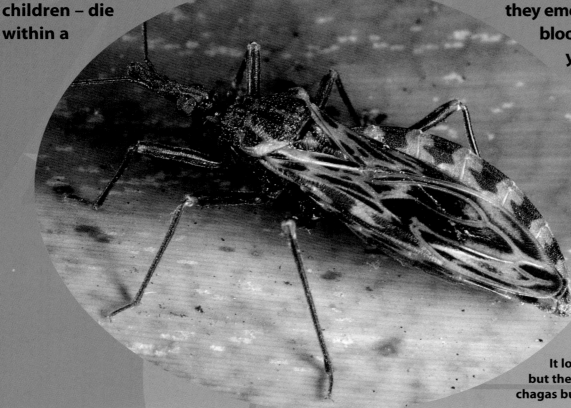

It looks harmless, but the bloodsucking chagas bug can be a killer.

BUG ALERT!

Deadly souvenir

Doctors reckon that about 18 million people now have chagas disease, and 100 million risk getting it. Many of these are travellers visiting Latin America for the first time on expensive vacation trips. Just sleeping in the wrong place can give you a souvenir you would rather do without. It can be cured, but only if it's treated quickly. Be careful out there.

The brown recluse spider: this shy creature has a vicious bite.

Eeeuch!

If you rummage around in a closet in any of the southern states of the USA, you might disturb a little brown spider with a dark violin-shaped mark on its back. It's called the brown recluse spider, and it has a habit of slipping into quiet, dry places such as cupboards and piles of clothes. It doesn't look like much, and you might not give it a thought unless you were seriously scared of spiders.

Here's a tip: be scared! That little spider has a bite like a rattlesnake. You may not notice it at first, but as the venom gets to work it starts to destroy the flesh around the pinprick wound. Gradually the flesh dies and starts to decay. It turns black, oozes pus and starts falling away. The decay can eat right down to the bone, covering an area the size of a saucer. Apart from getting a surgeon to cut it out with a knife, there's no cure.

Arachnophobia!

In 1993, a Californian woman bitten by a brown recluse spider suffered an allergic reaction that sent her into a coma for five months. Meanwhile, the venom gave her blood poisoning. This destroyed the flesh in her arms and legs, so doctors were forced to amputate them. When she woke up she had no arms or legs – and all because of a tiny spider bite. Brown recluse spider bites can cause horrible wounds, but they are rarely deadly. Of 126 people known to have been bitten in the USA, only six have died as a result.

What Lives Under the Floorboards?

How old is your house? If it's fairly modern it might have concrete floors. Nothing much can live there. But older houses have floors made of wooden boards nailed to beams. There's a gap beneath the boards, and down at ground level the gap can be huge. In some timber houses, the gap is open to the outside world, but usually it's a dark, mysterious, cobwebby void.

Some houses have mice and even rats living under the floor. Most of the resident animals are much smaller, though. Many are no trouble, but a few can bite or sting. Others attack the house itself by eating their way through the timber, and if nothing is done the whole floor can collapse in a cloud of dust.

Woodworm beetles like to set up home in your furniture.

Tick, tock

One of the more notorious timber-boring pests is the deathwatch beetle, which lives in expensive hardwoods like oak. Such timber is usually found only in ancient houses and churches, so the beetle is quite rare. It gets its name from the way the adults signal to one another in spring – by tapping their armoured heads against the timber walls of their tunnels: tap, tap, tap, like an old, ticking clock.

BUG ALERT!

Recycling gang

When a dead tree falls in the forest, the timber is recycled by insects with tough jaws and even tougher digestive systems. They can gnaw through dry wood, swallow it and convert the fibre into the sugars from which it is made. It's a useful trick, because it helps get rid of all that old dead wood.

Unfortunately, we have found other uses for dead wood, such as making floorboards. The last thing we need is a horde of hungry insects recycling them into sugar!

Tell-tale holes

Check out the floorboards of any old house, anywhere in the world, and you're almost bound to find the tell-tale holes made by woodworm. This insect is actually the grub of a small beetle called the furniture beetle because it also infests furniture. In fact, buying old furniture is one of the best ways of importing woodworm into your home.

Each beetle grub chews through the timber for up to four years, then turns into an adult and gnaws its way to the outside world. However, the beetles often return to lay their eggs in the exit holes. You can tell if there is a new generation eating the furniture because little heaps of fine powder appear under the holes. With floorboards, of course, the discovery could be more painful.

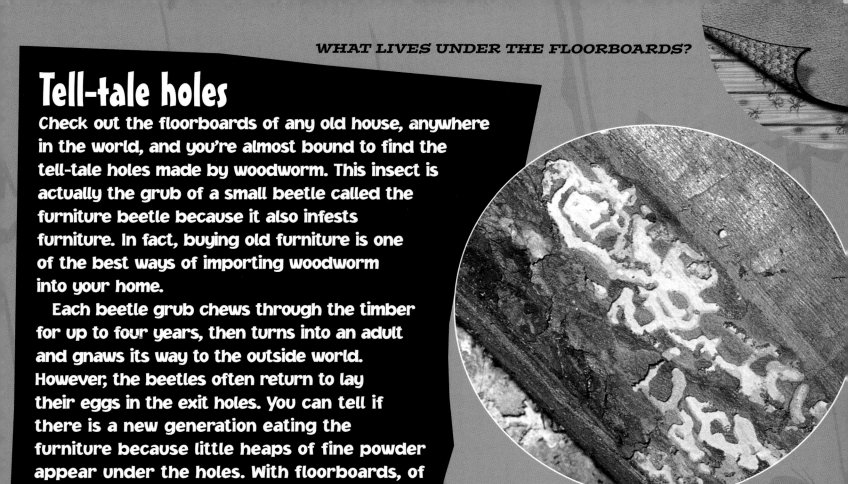

This is the work of a woodworm.

House-eating termites

Termites are the number one insect vandals. They live rather like ants – in massive colonies based around a single, massive queen. She lays thousands of eggs every day, which are looked after by small, blind, wingless workers. Some of the workers are specialized for defending the colony – they have enormous jaws, or nozzles on their heads that squirt nasty chemicals. The others build the nest and gather food. Each colony may have up to seven million termites, so they can gather an awful lot of food.

Like woodworm, termites can digest wood. Out in the forests, they attack dead trees, but if they get the chance they'll chew their way through floorboards, wooden walls, tables, pianos, books – in fact, whole houses! If you've got termites, then you've got trouble. BIG trouble!

The fearsome jaws of a termite soldier make short work of its enemies.

Hothouse ants

Most ants are just house visitors looking for a sugary meal, but some set up home right under the floorboards. One of the most troublesome is the pharoah ant, a tiny insect only 2 mm (0.1 in) long that lives in its millions, or more!

Once found only in hot climates, the pharoah ant has spread across the world to much cooler regions, where it must live in warm buildings to survive. Its favourite homes are hospitals, which are always warm and have big kitchens to raid for food, but it can turn up in any well-heated building. Being so tiny, the pharoah ant gets everywhere, and once it moves in it is almost impossible to shift.

Fire ants have fiery tempers.

Fiery imports

Fire ants were accidentally imported to the USA from South America in about 1940. Since then, they've overrun most of the southern states, living in huge colonies that can take over whole fields, and they often find their way into houses.

Fire ants are incredibly fierce, swarming over anyone who upsets them, biting and stinging them again and again. They've been known to kill small children and even a few adults. Never mess with fire ants!

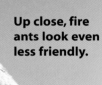
Up close, fire ants look even less friendly.

Ants a-plenty

All kinds of ants can move in under your floorboards if you give them good enough reason. In the USA alone, a house can be infested with pharoah ants, pavement ants, odorous house ants and carpenter ants, although not usually all at the same time. Mostly, these ants just feast on the food we leave lying around, but the carpenter ant, for one, is armed with big, sharp jaws – and isn't afraid to use them!

BUG ALERT!

Shy but deadly

The space beneath the floorboards could be a perfect home for the most notorious spider on Earth: the black widow. There are different types of black widow all over the world, including North and South America, southern Europe, South Africa, Australia and New Zealand. They are all fairly small, shiny black spiders with red markings. The tiny male is harmless, but the fat female is armed with one of the most deadly natural poisons known to man.

The black widow spider normally lives in a shed or outhouse, but a wooden frame house with a verandah and a gap beneath the floor is ideal black widow territory. She spins a rather untidy web and hangs upside down, waiting for prey. Normally, this spider is no trouble at all, and is actually rather shy – disturb a black widow in her web and she'll usually run for cover. But if she can't get away, she'll bite.

The female black widow: her reputation precedes her.

Killer bite

Black widow venom is a nerve poison. If the spider bites you, the poison makes your muscles go rigid. The pain is agonizing, you can't breathe properly and you feel faint, sick and dizzy. If you're strong and healthy, you'll probably get over it, but small children and old people often die. It's certainly the most deadly spider in North America. In one decade, 65 Americans died from spider bites, and 63 of these were caused by black widows. So, if you live in black widow country, watch out for shiny black spiders.

BUG ALERT!

What Lives in the Cellar?

If you've got a cellar, you probably don't go down there very often – that's what cellars are for. You might use it to store things you don't use but never get around to throwing away. The stacks of magazines, broken radios and abandoned exercise machines are left to gather dust in the dark. Occasionally, someone switches on the light, clumps down the stairs and disturbs the dust. Mostly, though, the animals have it to themselves.

You'd be amazed at the animals that move into cellars. If they can find a way in, red foxes or raccoons might decide to set up home and raise a family. If the cellar is damp enough, you may get toads and newts. Then there are mice, of course. But most of the creatures that live down in the cellar are of the smaller, leggier variety, and many have more legs than most of us would like.

Spider paradise

An undisturbed cellar is a paradise for spiders. Many spiders that once lived in caves and hollow trees find that houses – especially their cellars – make ideal substitutes. The most familiar of these are the house spiders: the rather hairy, leggy *Tegenaria* spiders that many people find so scary. They have become so attached to us that we have carried one of them, *Tegenaria domestica*, all over the world.

House spiders live in silken tubes attached to the triangular webs that drape every corner of the cellar, rushing out to snatch any insects that get trapped. They are really rather useful, catching flies and disposing of the furniture beetles whose woodworm young eat through the floorboards. So leave them alone! You probably wouldn't want to get too close to them anyway.

House spiders just want to catch flies.

Venomous exception

House spiders are big enough to bite you if they want to, but most varieties are fairly harmless. One exception is the hobo spider, which was brought to the north-western United States from western Europe some time before the 1930s. In Europe, it lives in fields, but in America it has moved into houses and is quite common in cellars. It behaves much like any other house spider and stays out of trouble if it can, but if it is trapped it can bite. Quite often, the spider just gives you a quick nip and runs away. If you're unlucky, though, it injects a shot of venom. This attacks the area around the bite, cutting off the blood supply so the flesh turns black and dies. It's like the bite of the brown recluse spider we met in the closet. Nasty!

Leggy male house spiders on walkabout often fall in the bath by mistake.

Armour-piercing fangs

Woodlice often live in cellars, and, where there are woodlice, there are likely to be woodlouse-eaters. These include centipedes and some beetles, but their most deadly enemy is the woodlouse spider. This sinister-looking, red-legged spider has a pair of extra-long pincer fangs, strong enough to pierce the woodlouse's protective armour. It hunts in the dark, and when it runs into a woodlouse it tilts its head to one side so it can stab one fang through its back and the other through its belly. It can bite you too, so watch out!

Out and about

Female house spiders usually stay in their webs, but during the mating season the long-legged males go walkabout. These are the spiders that charge across the floor, scattering humans in their wake, and get trapped in the bath when they fall in by mistake. You can tell a male because the short palps between his front legs have big 'boxing gloves' on the ends. But they're difficult to see when you're standing on a chair on the other side of the room.

BUG ALERT!

This woodlouse spider looks like it has been in the wars – it only has seven legs.

Roach raid

Apart from spiders and perhaps rats, the most unwelcome residents of dark, damp cellars are cockroaches. We've run into a few of these already, but so far we've managed to avoid the American cockroach. This burly beast is nearly always found in damp places, often occupying the basement while other types of cockroach entertain themselves upstairs.

Despite its name, the American cockroach lives all over the world, infesting drains and sewers where it picks up all kinds of vile infections. It eats pretty much anything, and there are stories of roaches emerging from city drains by the thousand on warm nights to raid restaurant kitchens. Think about that, the next time you visit your local burger bar.

A stinking, disease-ridden sewer is paradise to an American cockroach.

Creeping nightmare

One of the scariest living things to invade cellars isn't an animal at all. It's a fungus called dry rot. House-owners are terrified of dry rot: it creeps through the house timbers, digesting them like a plague of termites. Eventually the wood crumbles to dust and the house falls down. Dry rot gets its name from the way it can spread in timber that seems fairly dry. It can also spread over brickwork, plaster and even stone. Yet although the timber may seem dry, it must be a bit damp to support the fungus. If it can be permanently dried out – which is not always easy – the dry rot dies of thirst.

Shrimps out of water

If your cellar is the slightest bit damp, it is likely to be invaded by woodlice. These little creatures are not insects but crustaceans, relatives of shrimps, crabs and crayfish. Most crustaceans live underwater, but woodlice have found ways of surviving on land. If they venture too far from damp places, however, they dry out and die.

Woodlice feed mainly on dead and decaying plant material, which is why you often find them under the bark of logs cut for firewood, hiding from the light. A dark cellar suits them very well – provided they can find enough to eat.

Mass attack

One thing you wouldn't expect to find in a cellar is a nest of bees. Wild bees normally nest well away from people, in hidden cavities high off the ground. They wouldn't consider taking over part of anyone's house. Not unless they are killer bees . . . That's right: KILLER BEES! Killer bees were created in 1957 when a bunch of imported African bees escaped in Brazil and interbred with the local bees. The resulting 'Africanized' bees are far more aggressive than normal bees, attacking anyone that comes within sight of their nest. Their stinging attracts more bees, who join the attack. The combined effect of all those stings is lethal, and one victim was found with 8,000 stings in her dead body! They are among the most dangerous animals on Earth.

From Brazil, the killer bees moved north, right through Latin America to the southern states of the USA. So far they have killed almost 1,500 people. What makes them extra-dangerous is that they often nest near people – in walls, sheds and even disused cellars.

Watch out! There are killers on the loose!

Multi-legged monster

As if killer bees living in the cellar weren't enough, people living in tropical America may be visited by the awesome, venomous, giant centipede. This 33-cm (13-in) monster is the biggest and most dangerous of its kind! Since it can kill mice and toads with its curved fangs, it has good reason to slip into damp cellars in search of prey. Luckily, its bite is not deadly to people, but it is extremely painful.

Bee stings

- The venom of a killer bee is no more dangerous than the venom of an ordinary bee. It's just that you usually get at least ten times the dose, because you get at least ten times as many stings.
- Most victims of fatal killer bee attacks have been elderly. Younger people have survived more than 1,000 stings, although 500 would normally be deadly.
- African bees were originally brought to South America because they make three times as much honey as European-type bees in warmer climates.

BUG ALERT!

What Lives Under the Bed?

Take a look under your bed – carefully, just in case you disturb something nasty. . . . Apart from the old shoes you haven't worn for months, what else can you see? That's right: dust. Grey, fluffy dust blanketing the carpet and everything else. How does it get there?

You may not want to know this, but most of that dust is tiny bits of skin, which flake away throughout the day and night. And if it's your own bed you're looking under, it's probably your skin. To some microscopic creatures it's a rich source of food. They live under the bed – and in it – in their millions, and they are eaten by other, slightly larger creatures that attract spiders and other hunters. There's a whole zoo down there!

Dandruff? That's a tasty treat to a dust mite.

Little monsters

If you could look at some dust under a microscope, you'd find it was crawling with little monsters. These are dust mites: miniature relatives of spiders, with fat bodies, eight stumpy legs and a pair of pincer jaws. They feast on the skin flakes and fungi in the dust beneath the bed, and everywhere else in the house. There are at least 11 different species, and they live all over the world.

Dust mites are happiest in warm, slightly damp places, and prefer to be in houses with central heating and double glazing. The warmest, dampest place is your mattress, which also happens to collect a lot of skin flakes. So unless it's brand new, your bed is alive.

Dusty details

- Dust mites produce lots and lots of tiny droppings. If you suck up the dust with an average vacuum cleaner, the droppings pass right through the filter and are blasted into the air in a fine cloud. So don't breathe!
- Since they like it warm and damp, dust mites are rare in mountain countries like Switzerland. This is why the air there seems so clean and healthy.

Dust mites love to run around in your dirt.

Bedbug hunter

Not all bugs are bad news. One of the bedbug's deadly enemies is another bug called the masked bedbug hunter. This fearsome insect spears its victim with its long, sharp beak, then injects it with a paralysing venom that liquefies its flesh. The hunter sucks the resulting soup into its stomach, and when it is finished the bedbug is nothing but an empty husk. It's a useful bug to have around!

You are not alone

As you lie asleep in the dead of night, something may be sucking your blood. Like a miniature, creeping vampire, the bedbug emerges from its lair in the seams of the mattress and sniffs its way towards a sleeping victim. It slips its needle-like beak into a small blood vessel – often in its victim's throat, like any good vampire – and begins to suck. When it starts feeding, its body is wafer-thin, but by the time it creeps away ten minutes later it is bloated with blood. Your blood.

Bedbugs suck blood – so watch out!

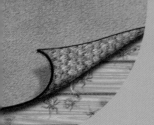

Sting in the tail

That's a real sting in the tail !

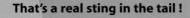

All the bugs, mites and other small creatures foraging through the dust under the bed attract several much bigger, meaner animals. In warmer countries these can include scorpions.

Although they look a bit like lobsters, scorpions are heavily armoured relatives of spiders. If you ever get close enough to count, you will find that a scorpion has eight legs, just like a spider. It also has a pair of powerful pincers that it uses to capture prey. As far as we are concerned, though, the bit to watch out for on a scorpion is the sting on the end of its long tail, which can be deadly.

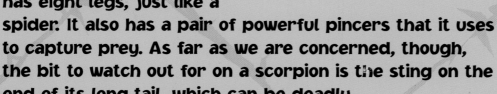

Nerve poison

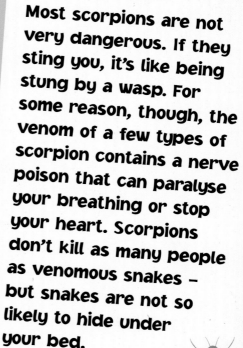

Most scorpions are not very dangerous. If they sting you, it's like being stung by a wasp. For some reason, though, the venom of a few types of scorpion contains a nerve poison that can paralyse your breathing or stop your heart. Scorpions don't kill as many people as venomous snakes – but snakes are not so likely to hide under your bed.

BUG ALERT!

Shake those shoes

Scorpions hate the light. Out in the wild they hide under stones during the day, but if a scorpion comes into your house looking for a juicy meal, it just creeps into the nearest dark crevice at daybreak. A shoe makes a perfect hideaway, until someone slips a foot into it. So if you are ever in a country where there are scorpions, watch out!

Wandering killer

If you're in South America or the southern states of the USA, be extra careful when you're poking about under the bed – you might come face to face with one of the most dangerous spiders in the world. It's called the Brazilian wandering spider, and although it normally hunts in the forest, it has a nasty habit of slipping into houses.

It might be big, but next to a huge, hairy tarantula the wandering spider looks fairly harmless. Don't be fooled! It has long fangs, which are connected to massive venom glands filled with a poison that is far stronger than that of any cobra.

A Brazilian wandering spider protecting its cocoon of unhatched spiderlings.

Spider snippets

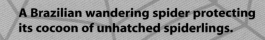

- The wandering spider deserves its deadly reputation. One of these spiders crept into the bed of two Brazilian children and killed them both while they slept.
- Unlike big tarantulas, the wandering spider can run fast, and may even jump up to 45 cm (1ft 6in) to pounce on its victims.
- Its huge venom glands are bigger than those of any other spider, including monster tarantulas.

Hitchhiker

The wandering spider gets its name from the way it wanders through the forest looking for prey instead of sitting in a web. It wanders much further than that, though. Sometimes it gets air-freighted to other parts of the world in cargoes of tropical fruit. It usually dies quite quickly if it lands somewhere cold, but a warm, centrally-heated house could suit it quite well. Unzipping a banana may never be the same again!

BUG ALERT!

What Lives on the Ceiling?

The ceiling looks like a pretty dull place to live. There doesn't seem to be much to eat, and there's nowhere to hide. It also has one very obvious drawback: it's the wrong way up. Many animals climb up to the ceiling, lose their grip and fall off. If you've ever found a spider in the bath, it probably fell from the ceiling, found itself in the slippery bath, and couldn't climb out.

Other creatures are better equipped for the upside-down life. Flies have sticky pads on their feet, so they can cling to the ceiling with no trouble at all. They use it as a refuge from their enemies, but then they don't reckon on visits from other acrobats such as geckos. These little lizards also have adhesive feet and make a living in warm countries by scuttling across ceilings and snapping up flies. And while some spiders fall off, others cling on – turning the ceiling into a deathtrap for unwary insects.

Packed lunch

One of the most cunning ceiling hunters is the daddy-long-legs spider, which lives in houses all over the world. With its extra-long, spindly legs and small body, it looks too fragile to be much of a killer, but it can kill and eat spiders much larger than itself.

It hangs in a flimsy-looking web in a corner of the ceiling, waiting for something to blunder into it. Then, keeping well clear of trouble, the spider uses its long legs to throw extra strands of silk over the struggling animal before it can tear itself free. When it is well entangled, the daddy-long-legs nips in, stabs it with its paralysing poison fangs and wraps it up for lunch.

This daddy-long-legs is actually a mummy-long-legs looking after her eggs.

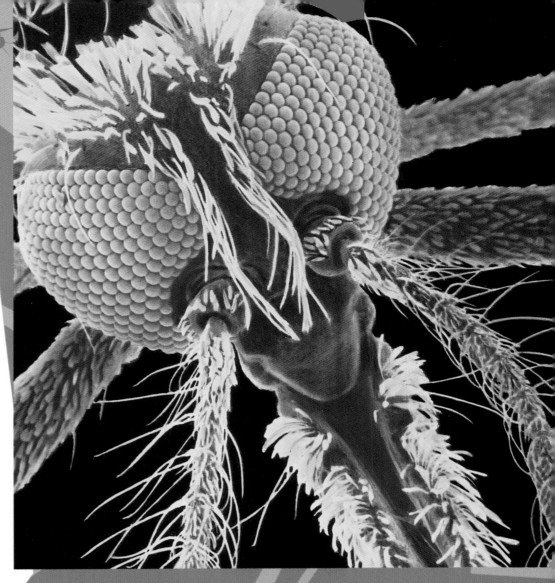

Blood meal

Among the many flies that cling to the ceiling are various midges and mosquitoes. You know about mosquitoes – they bite. They stab you with their hypodermic mouthparts and suck your blood. But maybe you didn't know that only female mosquitoes feed on blood, and the males are innocent vegetarians that drink nectar.

Female mosquitoes need blood to make their eggs. They track down their victims by sensing the air they breathe out, and by the heat of their bodies. So if that mosquito up on the ceiling is feeling hungry, it will find you even in pitch darkness.

Deadly

All mosquito bites are a pain, but some can be fatal. Many tropical mosquitoes carry serious diseases, including malaria and yellow fever. Malaria alone kills about 2 million people every year and it is becoming more difficult to cure. You can take pills that stop you catching it, but it's best not to get bitten in the first place.

Mozzy morsels

- The whine of a mosquito is the sound of its wings beating. Those of a female vibrate at a rate of 500 beats per second, but the male's vibrate even faster and whine at a higher pitch. So if you're musical you might be able to tell which is which – and whether you're likely to be bitten.

- Roughly half the world's human population risks catching malaria from infected mosquitoes. The disease is the biggest killer of children under five years old.

Hairy huntsman

In Europe, people often get frightened by spiders on the ceiling. They should visit Australia! Many of the spiders here are seriously big and hairy, and one of the biggest, hairiest and scariest is the huntsman, which likes to live in corners of the ceiling and catch any animals that come within reach.

The huntsman is also called the giant crab spider, because its legs curve forward so it looks rather like a crab. Those legs can span over 15 cm (6 in), and it has an equally massive set of poison fangs. Luckily, its poison is not the sort that is dangerous to people, and many Australians put up with it because it catches so many insect pests.

The mighty huntsman spider is a terrifying sight, but it's not as lethal as it looks.

High-speed hunter

One of the most spectacular hunters to get up near the ceiling is the outrageously leggy house centipede. Its body is fringed by 15 pairs of long legs, and the last pair is extended into extra-long whips for lassoing and snaring its insect prey. These are matched by a pair of whip-like antennae at the other end, so until it moves it's hard to tell which end is which.

When it does move, though, it really moves: zipping across the wall at amazing speed as it dashes after flies, crickets and cockroaches. A lazy insect like a bush cricket is easy prey and the centipede soon has it strapped up, ready for an injection of deadly venom from its poison fangs.

BUG ALERT!

Spider stowaway

The huntsman spider usually hunts by night, and it has a flattened body so it can hide behind the loose bark of forest trees during the day. In towns it sometimes finds its way into a car, climbs up and hides behind one of the sun visors. You can imagine what happens when the driver flips down the visor and a giant hairy spider falls out. It may not have a lethal bite, but it can still be deadly.

Filthy flies

Wherever there are houses, there are houseflies. They've been living alongside humans for thousands of years, eating our food and breeding in the garbage and dirt that we spread about us. Even worse, they carry disease organisms from the dirt to the food, and these diseases kill millions of children every year.

In modern cities we've got the filth problem fairly well controlled, so houseflies are not such a health hazard. They still invade our houses, though, and if you try to swat one it's likely to fly up and land on the ceiling. Up there it's usually well out of our range, but a friendly spider might help you out.

Houseflies may clean themselves a lot, but they need to. They live in rubbish dumps, and one housefly can carry over a million germs.

Trick landing

How does a fly land upside down on the ceiling? In a bid to find out, a scientist once filmed a housefly with a high-speed camera. The film showed it zooming toward the ceiling at full throttle, but just before impact it reached out with its front legs and slammed on the brakes. The fly then grabbed the ceiling and swung up like a gymnast to cling on with its sticky little feet. It's a neat trick.

Strange but true: the plume moth

Feathers and spurs

Among the creatures sitting on your ceiling you might find a plume moth. The wings of this weird little insect are split into separate parts that look like feathers. There are five on each side, although normally you can see only two. Its legs are strange, too, with long spurs at the joints that give them an odd, twiggy look. Quite why it has evolved in this curious way is anyone's guess.

What's Buzzing Around the Light?

If you leave a light on near an open window on a summer's evening, it will attract all kinds of night-flying insects. It's possible that they mistake it for the Moon, trying to use it for navigation. If it really were the Moon, an insect could keep a straight course by flying at a fixed angle to it. But with an electric light, the insect ends up buzzing uselessly around and around, closer and closer, and risks being burnt by the hot lamp.

Not all the insects buzzing around the light are night-flyers, though. A commotion in the lampshade could be a sleepy fly that has become confused by the light. If you switch it off, the noise will probably stop as the fly settles back in the dark.

Moths fly at night but love the light.

Whirring wings

The most enthusiastic light visitors are moths: night-flying equivalents of the butterflies that brighten up the garden by day. They come out at dusk to sip nectar from night-scented flowers like honeysuckle, but some get confused by the light. They fly up against the window on whirring wings and, if they get the chance, they come right into the house. Since they fly in the dark, most moths have no use for the glowing colours sported by butterflies, and many are a drab brown for daytime camouflage. The garden tiger moth is a dazzling exception, with brightly coloured wings that act as a warning to birds that it has a vile taste.

The garden tiger moth looks pretty but tastes pretty awful.

Heavy armour

Sometimes a really alarming creature hurtles through an open window towards the light. Big, heavily armoured beetles often set off on cross-country flights at nightfall, droning across the landscape like bombers on an air raid. They are attracted to light like moths and if one of these heavyweights manages to get in the house, it's like coming under attack.

Beetles have tough wing cases to protect their thin, delicate wings. In flight, the wing cases hinge out from their bodies like open doors, and it's amazing that they can fly at all.

Clumsy cranefly

One of the most irritating insect visitors is the leggy, clumsy cranefly. It's really just an overgrown gnat, but its brain seems to have stayed gnat-sized.

The cranefly blunders around the light with its legs dangling, bumping into the lampshade and crash-landing in awkward places. Many adult craneflies don't feed at all and have very short lives, so maybe a brain would be a pointless luxury.

It may look like a giant mosquito, but the blundering cranefly is totally harmless.

Scary stripes

The cranefly terrifies some people because it looks like a flying spider. Striped hoverflies can be scary too, because they look like wasps. This is no accident: their stripes are intended to trick their enemies into thinking they have a sting in their tail. Don't be fooled!

If you look closely at a hoverfly, you can see that it's just a bluebottle in disguise. Like all true flies it has only two wings instead of four, but the second pair have become little 'balancers' that help control its flight. They certainly work for hoverflies, which can hang in the air like tiny hummingbirds.

What Lives in the Attic?

Some houses have really tidy attics. They've been turned into rooms that you can live in, with proper stairs and windows. These are not real attics.

A real attic is a roof space full of old boxes, broken furniture, camping gear and mysterious tin trunks. It's dusty, dirty and dark, with huge cobwebs draped between the rafters and nasty things lurking in the corners.

Some quite big animals can get into the attic. A squirrel may sneak in through a hole, and birds such as swallows can raise families in nests built on the timber beams. Bats love attics, slipping between the tiles to roost in the rafters. But most of the creatures living in the attic are much smaller – and a lot more troublesome.

Museum beetles like something old rather than something new.

Dusty feast

The strange things that end up in attics can provide some insects with a real banquet. Stuffed animals, old woollen rags and bits of carpet are a feast for the young of the museum beetle. They are able to eat dead animal matter such as dried skin, hair and scales, and convert it into useful food. They can be serious pests in museums, gradually reducing valuable specimens to dust, and they'll do the same in your attic if they get the chance.

Golden horde

At the end of summer, the attic can attract swarms of flies with golden fur. They are called cluster flies because they crowd together in dense clusters to spend the winter in sheltered corners. In spring they emerge and fly outside to lay their eggs on earthworms, which are then eaten alive by their maggots.

Heart-stopper

For most of us, a dusty, neglected attic means just one thing: spiders! All those cobwebs must have been made by something, and if they're all occupied, then you definitely don't want to visit the attic ever again.

In fact, spider silk is so durable that an abandoned cobweb can last for years – long after its builder has moved on – so the webs were probably made by just one or two spiders. Even so, you might not want to meet one of them face to face. It might be a cardinal spider, the biggest of the European house spiders, whose occasional high-speed dashes across the carpet can be frightening.

Spitting spiders catch their prey by spitting on it, hence their name!

Nailing a meal

The little yellow-and-black spitting spider is found in attics all over the world. Slowly stalking up to a fly, it suddenly fires a mixture of venom and glue from its fangs. The mixture sets into sticky, poisoned threads that glue themselves to the first thing they touch. As it fires, the spider vibrates its fangs from side to side, creating zig-zag strands that nail the fly to the floor. After that, it's lunch!

Pesky mites

If there are birds nesting under the eaves, or even in the attic itself, their nests are likely to be infested with tiny mites. They suck the birds' blood, but if the birds move out (and who could blame them?) the mites have to look elsewhere. They have been known to go on safari through houses, swarming down walls and even into beds to find a meal. It can be an itchy, scratchy experience, and the mites are so small they usually get away with it.

BUG ALERT!

Unwelcome tenants

If you hear a low buzzing coming from the attic, it could be one of two things: either it's a low-flying helicopter or you've got wasps.

Wasps are really quite useful insects because they kill huge numbers of flies, caterpillars and other pests to feed their young. The most efficient of these hunters live in colonies, with a single queen laying the eggs and all the others – the workers – collecting food and building the nest. Normally they build it in a hollow tree or hanging from a branch, depending on the type of wasp, but if they get the chance they may move into your attic.

Wasps tend to get possessive about the space they live in. It's *their* attic, not yours, and if you go up there they don't like it. If you get too close, the workers stream out to defend their queen, stinging for all they're worth.

Paper wasps chew up wood to make their nest.

Paper palace

Wasps build their nests from paper – not normal paper, but then it hasn't been bleached white and rolled out by a machine. The wasps make it by scratching wood from trees and fences and chewing it to a pulp. They use the pulp to make layers of hexagonal, honeycomb-like cells, often covered with an outer protective 'envelope'. It dries into a paper palace for their queen and her young.

This common wasp is a social insect, but it also has a lot of chores to do – like looking after its queen.

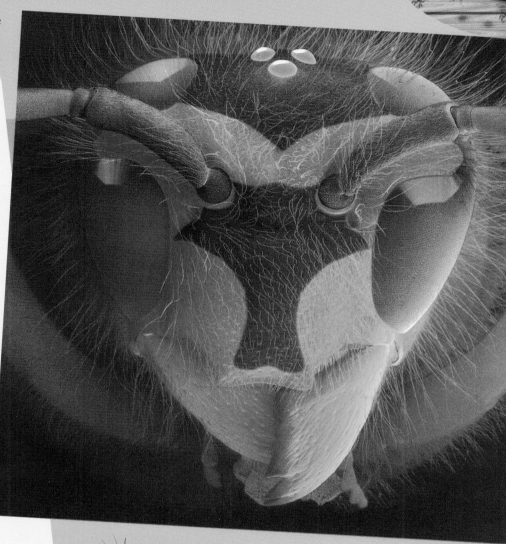

Sleeping queens

In cold regions like northern Europe, the winter kills off all the worker wasps and their nest is deserted. The young queens survive, though, by hiding in sheltered crevices. After sleeping through the winter, they emerge in spring to start new colonies.

Attics are ideal places for queen wasps to hide. They slip through gaps in the tiles and creep into old boxes and other cosy corners. They're harmless, as long as they are not disturbed, and in the spring they usually just fly away.

Stinging time

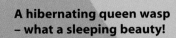

- Adult wasps feed on nectar, ripe fruit and other sweet things, which is why they are such picnic pests. They feed insects to their young, though.

- At the end of summer, the queen stops laying eggs and the worker wasps are left with no mouths to feed. They have nothing better to do than hang around making nuisances of themselves, and this is when you are most likely to be stung.

BUG ALERT!

A hibernating queen wasp – what a sleeping beauty!

Quiz Pages

Baffling Bugs

These pictures all show bits of bugs. Can you name them?

Animal Anagrams

Try unscrambling these jumbled-up words to find out which bugs and microbes are lurking on this page.

teebel

trimeet

ticker

salin

lugs

digem

leaf

frygleen

gant

mowrokob

bitefarr

drydabli

Having a bit of trouble? Are the answers bugging you? See page 46 for some help.

Minibeast Mindbenders

Can you name a creature that:

1 is a ceiling hunter that likes to wrap up its lunch in silk?
2 has many pairs of legs, making it one of the fastest insects around?
3 looks like a tiny armadillo?
4 has a mark in the shape of a violin on its back?
5 is a relative of spiders and has a pair of pincer jaws?
6 has been known to live inside a television?
7 feeds on nectar and fruit and can live in your attic?
8 has a heavily armoured body and a deadly tail?
9 is the number one insect vandal that will eat any dead wood for lunch?
10 is a flying bug that carries disease organisms from dirt to your food?

How many did you score?

1-4 It's a good start! Now go back and do some more reading.
5-7 Great! You've certainly learned a lot.
8+ Excellent! You must be the world's expert on what lives under your carpet, in your larder and even on your ceiling!

Nasty Numbers

Can you remember the answers to these nauseating number puzzles?

1 How many legs does the common centipede have?
a 50
b 100
c 30
d 4

2 How many times per second does the female mosquito flap its wings?
a 1
b 500
c 5
d 5,000

3 A tiny cat flea can jump up to how many times its length?
a 5 times
b 50 times
c 100 times
d 250 times

4 A huntsman spider's legs can span up to how far?
a 5 cm
b 15 cm
c 10 cm
d 30 cm

5 The wandering spider can jump up to how far?
a 20 cm
b 30 cm
c 45 cm
d 60 cm

6 How many years has the cockroach been in existence?
a 300
b 3,000
c 3,000,000
d 300,000,000

Answers

Nasty Numbers

1 c 2 b
3 d 4 b
5 c 6 d

Minibeast Mindbenders

1 Daddy-long-legs spider
2 Centipede
3 Pillbug
4 Brown recluse spider
5 Dust mite
6 Brown-banded cockroach
7 Wasp
8 Scorpion
9 Termite
10 Housefly

Animal Anagrams

ladybird

firebrat

bookworm

gnat

flea

midge

greenfly

slug

snail

cricket

termite

beetle

Baffling Bugs

1 Bedbug
2 Pillbug
3 Fire ant
4 Recluse spider
5 Termite
6 Funnelweb spider
7 Huntsman spider
8 Centipede

46

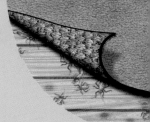

Index